MY
JOURNEY

MY
JOURNEY

A STORY OF A SERVANT AND SOLDIER OF CHRIST

BROTHER FRANK CANDLISH
GOD'S STRUGGLER

MY JOURNEY
A STORY OF A SERVANT AND SOLDIER OF CHRIST

iUniverse books may be ordered through booksellers or by contacting:

iUniverse
1663 Liberty Drive
Bloomington, IN 47403
www.iuniverse.com
844-349-9409

Because of the dynamic nature of the Internet, any web addresses or links contained in this book may have changed since publication and may no longer be valid. The views expressed in this work are solely those of the author and do not necessarily reflect the views of the publisher, and the publisher hereby disclaims any responsibility for them.

Any people depicted in stock imagery provided by Getty Images are models, and such images are being used for illustrative purposes only. Certain stock imagery © Getty Images.

ISBN: 978-1-6632-1197-2 (sc)
ISBN: 978-1-6632-1198-9 (e)

Library of Congress Control Number: 2021900367

Print information available on the last page.

iUniverse rev. date: 01/12/2021

INTRODUCTION

All who have asked our Lord Jesus Christ into their lives, and have continued that walk throughout their days, have a story to tell.

Some stories need to be told. Some stories should be read, and others just read for reading sake. That will be determined by you the reader.

I have been told by some folks that I should write an account of my life and journey with Christ. So, to quote that old-time honored hymn, *"This is my story. This is my song. Praising my Savior all the day long"!* Here it goes!

**"People who know their God, shall be strong and do exploits! "(Daniel 11:32)

DEDICATED TO

Janet Berger-Candlish: My wife *of almost 4 decades, friend, mother of our 4 children, grandma to our 9 grandchildren, managed our household, Listened to my story's countless times.*

Mary Claudine Candlish (my mother): *Who supported and prayed for me in all my missions from God.*

Pastor Larry and Pat Basnett: *Who prayed and stood with me from the beginning.*

Robert Valadez: *Who first suggested I write a book and share my stories. When I responded with: There have been numerous who have similar stories to tell. He responded," Everyone's story is different!"*

Rebecca Cojocaru: *(a Romanian University Student): Told me she found my stories "inspiring".*

A Christian U.S. Customs Official *(Los Angeles Airport): After an exchange, suggested I write this book.*

Mike and Carol Walker: *For their editing skills and suggestions.*

Also, to those whom I have never met in person, but as a result of the missions I was sent on by God, somehow impacted their lives, and ultimately influenced others in their walk and life with Him.

*** *All Holy Bible quotes are from "The Living Bible", Tyndale publish House.*

CHAPTER 1

MY EPIPHANY

I was born and raised in the San Fernando Valley, California. Growing up I spent most of my time at a non-denominational fellowship "Osborne Neighborhood Church". Pastor Jack Stiles was the founding pastor. Prior to starting this church from the ground, he was affiliated with a large Pentecostal denomination. Pastor Stiles was booted out when he declared he believed one could be filled with the Holy Spirit and not have to speak in tongues. In all fairness, it should be noted neither was he against the gift of tongues either.

The church had a lot to offer to all age groups and had various music opportunities from elementary age to adults. My parents were active in the church and required us to participate in the various choirs and youth groups. Sundays were anything but a day of rest, with dad singing in a quartet in the first service, then both of my parents sang in the choir in the late service. We came home, and then returned for youth choir, youth groups, and yes, you guessed it, Sunday night service.

Despite this, like all organizations, there were the favorites who were called up on for special parts in the music, and the youth program. Ya! you probably guess it, I was one of the guys who spend most of the time on the outside, hoping to be included on the inner circles sometime or another. When I was fifteen years old, I inherited the church janitor job from my older brother. It was required I be there after school on Tuesdays to clean the sanctuary, bathroom, and nursery. On Saturdays I cleaned the sanctuary, and the Sunday school rooms across the parking lot. Here I learned to serve. For all this, I was paid $5.00 a week. Even for that time, it was not very much, but I learned to serve...

Our church always had a winter camp for its youth and a summer camp in Kings Canyon. A bunch of volunteers from the church put up the tents, laid out the kitchen, and a place to have our meetings. I will never forget the Pastor's wife, Mrs. Stiles (we were not allowed to call her Patti). She accompanied the guitar players on a little pump organ. The meeting areas had folding chairs and a bunch of Coleman white gas lanterns. Was a great atmosphere to learn about God.

Some of the highlights during the week, were the mandatory quiet times on the King River, and walks we all took on the road under the stars. Of course, there was always the joys of the bears raiding the garbage cans at night. During these times, I believe just about all of us had some sort or another of unique spiritual experiences during these camps.

I seem to notice a pattern over the years. Most of us would get super charged, accept or rededicate our lives to Christ, get "filled with the Holy Spirit", get baptized if needed, and be "super spiritual" for a time, and then alas; subsequently return to the old person we use to be.

These times were also not the best to be growing up in. Instead of being kids growing up and dealing with the normal challenges of adolescent life, we were surrounded by chaos in our society. There were civil rights marches taking place all over the country, usually accompanied by riots and destruction. We live on the out skirts of a black community. At that time, radical blacks were threatening to invade white neighborhoods. I recall my mom assigning us a corner of the house to defend in the event this threat was carried out. Heck, we did not hate anyone because of their color! Additionally, the big hippy movement was taking place around the country, that was changing the standards of morality and the way we lived and believe. Further, the war in Vietnam was in progress, there were protests all around us. If that was not enough, to broaden the gap of insecurity, during high school, the teachers decided to walk off the job and go on strike.

All this effected my life growing up, in addition to problems within our home, and confusing doctrine taught by well-meaning folks. Such as God choosing who would be saved, and Jesus saved us from sin, but because of our "sinful nature", we could not help but continue to sin. We were told if we were filled the spirit and spoke in tongues, we would be "super Christians". Additionally, I was told by well-meaning persons, the Father, Son, and Holy Spirit were the same person. The explanation to justify this was to compare them to an ice cube, and an egg.

All of this was very confusing to me and caused me to wonder if God really existed. But to be on the safe side, every night I would ask for forgiveness for my sins just in case I died that night. To be honest I really did not know if I had sinned or not. Just covering all bases. If God did exist, the last place I wanted to end up was in hell. During this time, I also started dabbling in things I had no business being a part of.

It appeared those around me, did not recognize what was going on inside of me. I was pretty much felt I was on my own, looking for intelligent answers, and to fill the void for the need for love and acceptance. (A terrible place to be in during the adolescent years and very alone. Hope others do not have to go through this).

On a night in February 1972, all of this came to a climax! I was home alone for a change. I was confused in my life and did not like where it was it headed. In desperation I prayed to God. I asked Him if there was something more to Christianity than I knew. God's small quiet voice responded to my cry and said, "Yes Frank, there is. There is getting to know me."

For some unknown reason, these were the words I needed to hear. It met spending time with God, listening to Him, studying His word with Him, and developing a real relationship with Him. Up to this point from what I was taught, getting to know God was to ask Jesus in our hearts, ask forgiveness for sin, get baptized, pray, and read the Bible.

That night I called Larry and Pat Basnett, my youth ministers. They were at the same choir dinner my parents were at. But the person that answered the phone sensed something seriously was going on in my life and told me come over. She was babysitting the youth minister's children.

3

She had come through the Hollywood modeling scene and gave her heart to Jesus.

I hopped on my ten-speed bike and drove through the dark. I talk with her (cannot recall her name) and shared what was going on. Ultimately Larry and Pat came home, and we continued the conversation. They prayed with me and I gave my life back to Jesus (was told I did that at three years old). Larry called my parents and gave me a ride home. Normally I would by been chastised for riding in the dark by my dad. I did not talk with him that night, but I think he understood.

At my next appearance at church, word got around about my experience. Some came up and patted me on the back and congratulated me, but none took the time to help me get on with my journey. A week or so later, I found myself doing some of the same stuff I should not have been doing. It was like I ran into a tree and suddenly realized what I was doing. Here I had asked God to help me, gave Him my life, and was screwing up already. I stopped doing it immediately, asked God for forgiveness, and moved on. This was my first lesson in learning sin was a choice. A choice I no longer wanted to have as a part of my life with God.

CHAPTER 2

THE BEGINNING OF MY JOURNEY

T hings did start changing in my life as I daily prayerfully read the Bible considering God's relationship with man, waited on Him, and started listening instead of doing all the talking. I started to improve in school and started doing homework. One of my schoolteachers commented to me, that had I done this quality of work sooner, I would be an "A" student.

I did manage to barely graduate from high school with a "C" average. My thoughts started to turn towards my future. My attention turned towards to a four-year Christian College, who happen to have a football team. I also asked about that in my inquiry. Before I knew it, I received a letter from the coach with an interview scheduled. My dad was elated as he loved sports and was unable to participate due to an injury that occurred to him when he was young in a doctor's office.

My father accompanied me to the interview. The first question the coach asked was, "Did you bring some playing films with you"? When I explained my short-lived football career in high school and how I ended up meeting with him, he looked perplexed. Although short lived, I was good at the sport. I shared with him about my conversion months previously and the changes that had taken place in my life. I articulated that I believe I could be an asset to the team

The look on his face made it obvious what he was thinking hard. He finally took a deep breath, and said, "OK! I will give you a chance and send you a letter of acceptance and instruction." My dear father was excited! This opportunity also came with a scholarship and the coach mentioned the possibility of joining the wrestling team in the off season for another scholarship opportunity.

When I got back home, I immediately developed a workout program that included weightlifting, protein drinks, and the cursed running to build strength and endurance. I hated running! After the workout and running every day, a nice hot shower, I admit, I felt rather good.

Then came a change I did not see coming. Prior to reporting to football camp, I visited my grandparents at their vacation home at Lake Isabella. My Christian grandparents were the greatest!!

One of the greatest blessings a young man could have.

My dear sweet grandma had a three-wheel bicycle with a basket on the back. She would ride in front of me while I ran with her through the tract their home was located. Must have been quite a sight. During this time, I met some local kids from the neighborhood and got to know them. They had screwed up lives, were trying to make it, but did not have Jesus. They opened their hearts to me and shared their problems and concerns. I told them about Jesus and what had happened in my own life. On my drive back home, there was a heavy burden on my heart for them and I prayed intensely for them. While driving through the town of "Pumpkin Patch", outside of Bakersfield, I experienced again the small quiet voice of God, telling me He was calling me to work with kids like that.

It was a very real experience. Subsequently, I concluded I should drop the football scholarship, get some training and go back to Lake Isabella and open a Christian Coffee House or something similar, in order to reach out to the kids up there.

My poor dad, when I told him about this, he was disappointed and somewhat leery. His son was passing up a great opportunity to chase the wind. He did not put it in those words, but he also said it was my decision and life. Dad also loved the Lord and wanted us to follow His direction. I drove to my church and found dear pastor Larry in his office. I shared with him about my experience and the need for some training. He had just received a brochure from Youth with a Mission advertising a school that was to start in a short time. The school was just minutes driving time from my home.

I arranged an appointment to talk to the director of the school. I explained to him what had happened to me and my desire for an education to be equipped for ministry. He said the school was called "Mobile Training Team School". The curriculum included three months classroom time, and one-month field training in Hawaii. After that, students were to be divided into teams like Jesus' disciples, given a van, $100 cash and a first engagement booked to teach weeklong discipleship classes for a total of five months.

I was accepted in the school, given special permission to reside at my home in the valley, and commute daily.

Prior to starting the school, Pastor Larry told me about a "Basic Youth Conflict" seminar that was coming up soon. He believed I might benefit from it. A group from my church was going so I could catch a ride with them.

I imagined a small building with several people participating in it. Wow was I surprised! It was held in the Long Beach Convention Center and was packed. We were given a thick syllabus and spent all day through the evening with breaks and lunch for 5 days. The speaker was a fellow named Bill Gothard.

For the first time in my life, I was given Scriptural instruction and hands on guidelines. Regarding things I was told a Christian should be and do but was never given any tools. This seminar held my attention all week long. I was also doing something I had never done before; I was taking detailed-"copious notes" (to quote Ernest P. Werle).

Some of the topics included Clear conscience Christianity, restitution, forgiveness, submission in the family, consequences of rebellion, chain of command, seeking God, building a family, finances, and so on and so on. Subsequently I realized there was some need in my life to seek forgiveness to those I had previously wronged and hurt, and that some restitution had to be made. These acts of reconciliation made me think twice before committing them again.

The Sunday before I was to start the school, my church hosted an Eastern European mission. A film of the underground church was shown. I remember watching the film and the Lord spoke to me saying, "Someday you will go there." I was seventeen years old at the time and thought. Ya!! When I am older and mature. (Who would have thought nine months later??)

In no time at all, the Mobile Training School started. This was the beginning of doors to open that I could have never imagined happening with my walk with God.

I never did get back to Lake Isabella to start that work I assumed I was being called to.

CHAPTER 3

WALKING THE HALLS OF EDUCATION

I will never forget driving to school on my first day in my trusted ole red 1963 Chevy Nova. It was a car my dad helped me find I purchased for $300. It was anything but a chick magnet, but thanks to my dad, I found a good-solid car that served me well for many years.

The class size was about thirty students. They came from all over the United States, that included two farm girls from Nebraska.

The day started off with a devotional and we were split up into small intercessory prayer groups. Intercessory prayer was one of the many important items I learned during this school. I learned prayer was pretty much the foundation of any calling or work that God would call you to. We learned to wait on God in silence and allow the Holy Spirit to show us to *"pray as we ought"* in detail rather than second guessing ramblings. We were also encouraged" to be willing to be an answer to our prayers" if so, directed by God.

Many speakers came to instruct us, and I learned about developing a personal life with God, discipleing others, seeking God, learning to hear His voice, guidance, mission work, trusting God, as previously mentioned

9

intercessory prayer, and much- much more. It was exciting for me to learn the "letter of the law, as well as the spirit of the law", to develop skills to share this with others. One of the greatest challenges laid before us was to learn to share and speak publicly. At the beginning of each week of the school, we were given a topic to study and prepare a "sermon". On Saturday nights we would gather for a formal meal of good food and worship, called a "Love Feast". Towards the end, several were called on to deliver their talks. No one knew who would be called until that night I will never forget the night I was called upon. I cannot recall the topic, but I remember having a lot of notes and delivering my talk in five minutes. Now that I am older and have had so much learning with God and experiences, I could easily go two hours if allowed.

The classroom time ended sometime at the end of November. Most of the students went home for Thanksgiving, and some of them went ahead to the Town of Redwood City, California, where we had a field trip and outreach of sorts at a Christian Coffee House.

A couple of my friends and fellow students resided in the San Fernando Valley. Most of us had never flown or taken a train before. So, we decided the day after thanksgiving we would take the Amtrak train to San Jose and catch up with the school. That was quite an adventure for us traveling on the train through small communities and along the coast of California. I bought a bunch of turkey sandwiches made from leftovers from Thanksgiving dinner. I had a great time at the outreach. But I was really looking forward to the field trip in Hawaii.

The trip to Hawaii was my first time to seeing God provide for plane tickets. I learned early in ministry, that as a "Servant and Soldier" of God, if He were to send me somewhere that He would provide. When given the opportunity to share in my local church or wherever when God was leading me, I never asked for money, but rather for their prayers. God always provided for me just like he promised.

On the day we flew to Hawaii, I will never forget two of the students did not have money for their tickets. However, in faith, they came to the airport anyway. Most of us had already boarded, when these two came running on the plane just prior to take off. While waiting at the airport a Christian brother came in and handed them the funds they needed. God spoke to him to pay for their tickets and to get to the airport to carry out his mission. I remember saying to one of the girls, "You made it". She replied, "Did you not think God would provide for us"?

There was this cute but true saying we learned, "Where God guides, He provides"!

Hawaii was adventure for me. But lessons of learning to work as a team, learning to minister in churches as a group and individually was quite a challenge. I will never forget the lizards (Geckos) that inhabited the buildings and chirped during church services.

One non-spiritual matter I will never forget was walking to a refreshment stand in the village we stayed at. There was this dropped dead exquisite-beautiful girl working there with the most beautiful brown hair, killer eyes, and wore a blue muu-muu dress. But the most outstanding character of her looks was her bushy hairy arm pits. That is most likely why I never forgot her.

The Hawaiian trip was a learning experience for me, as I learned to pray, work on a ministry team, and develop public speaking skills,

While in the classroom, there was talk about an outreach (Mayday outreach) in the Communist Soviet Union, where a group of students were gathering to openly share the Gospel with the Russian people, to encourage the underground church (to let them know they had not been forgotten) and bring proof to the free world there was not "religious freedom" in the communist world. This part of the world has always been heavy on my heart. So, I was praying about it and seeking God's guidance if I was to be a part of it. This outreach was not to be taken lightly. It could result in physical injury or imprisonment.

Upon return to the mainland, we were divided into teams and sent on our way. I was blessed to have a team leader with experience. I Learned a lot. Our team seemed to have a lot of opportunities for ministry. The "Mayday Outreach" to the Soviet Union was quickly approaching. I was still seeking God at this time if I was supposed to be a part of this outreach.

One day my confirmation from God came in a most unlikely way. My team was in the town of Eureka, California. We were on our way out the door to go share at the local university's Bible Study.

The phone rang and it was for me. I was thinking who would be calling me here? It was my youth Pastor Larry. He told me the deacons at our church wanted to help me with finances for the "Mayday Outreach". It was the very last day to confirm my participation with a deposit. I told Pastor Larry to contact the local mission office for information how to send the deposit. Coincidence??? Ya Right!!! I was able to share at the college Bible study that day with a fresh personal experience to share of God's provision. At this time, I knew God was sending me (insignificant me) to a far land to make a difference.

Two others of my team members were going to be a part of that outreach. It seemed like a short time before we returned to Los Angeles, to prepare and leave for our trip to the Soviet Union.

CHAPTER 4

FIRST OVERSEAS MISSION

The day of departure finally arrived. Here I am, just turned 18 years old and heading to the Communist Soviet Union for my first overseas mission. My family, and a bus load from my church came to pray and send me off at the airport. They sang a song for me; *"It is the Lord who goes before you. He will be with you. It is the Lord who goes before you. He will not fail nor forsake you. It is the Lord who goes before you!!!"* Everyone gathered around us, prayed for us, and sent us on our way. Soon we boarded the Pan American Boeing 747 and were on our way, not knowing if or when we would return. I felt blessed to be in the presence of several other brothers who were experienced in foreign travel. Upon arrival in London, while landing I could see Buckingham Palace and the infamous Big Ben. After going through immigration, we boarded a bi-level bus, got off, went underground to catch a subway (the tube).

After getting to our stop, we got off, went up top to the street, walked to the house where we gathered to prepare for the mission. The neighborhood looked like something I had seen in movies with multilevel homes. We were greeted at the door, took care of business, and escorted to our room on the third or fourth floor. I immediately went to sleep. One serious time change!!

The following days we met for prayer, briefings, getting acquainted, and personal preparation. This outreach took a lot of planning as there was fifty of us. Easter fell during this time. What a blessing it was to spend Easter in England with brothers and sisters from different parts of the world.

We were assigned to a team and duties to perform during our travels through Europe, Scandinavia, Finland, and into the Soviet Union. My assignment was to help set up camp, tear it down, and help unpack and pack the vans.

We were to pose as students coming to observe the big celebration of Communism on Mayday in Red Square in Moscow. We were to receive materials previously smuggled in, to hand out when we got there and share Christ.

Our day for departure finally arrived. We drove to Brighton, England, set up camp, shared a meal, and it begin to rain. There was a nearby old pub from the days of Shakespeare who allowed us to hold a meeting in a back room. We were further briefed and prayed together.

The following day, the weather cleared up and we drove to catch a hovercraft to cross the English Channel to France. While driving through northern France we saw where the allied troops invaded at Normandy and viewed numerous Grave sites of allied troops.

We drove through Denmark into Sweden where we caught a Ferry across the Baltic Sea to Finland.

We slept on the deck of the ferry on benches that were covered with overhead heaters.

Upon arrival in Finland, we stayed at a Christian accommodation. We were further briefed, put aside Items (i.e., Bibles, crosses, etc.) that would identify us as Christians and blow our cover.

The following day we prayed, packed up the vans, and headed to the Soviet Border. There were gun towers, tall fences with razor sharp and electric wire, and a mine field. We were greeted by armed soldiers who collected our passports and visas. After a rather lengthy process we were allowed to enter the Soviet Union.

Our first stop was at an In-tourist office to clear up some wrong dates on our itinerary that would allow us in Moscow on Mayday and we pick up our two tour guides. We were shown many historical places before arriving at our hotel outside of Moscow.

It had appeared our itinerary had been worked out. On the day before Mayday, we had had finished dinner and our tour guide stood up to announce our agenda for the following day. A trip to Moscow was not mentioned. Our leader stood up and wanted to know why Moscow was not there. Then rest of us stood up demanding to know why we were not going for the Mayday celebration in Moscow. The tour guide said let us go to the in house Intourist office at the Hotel and get this worked out once and for all. We marched into the office in unison, phone calls were made, and it was clear we were not wanted in Red Square on the following day.

The local police chief marched into the office and demanded we park our vans in a locked garage. However, the garage was so compact our vans would not fit. When it became clear we were not going to be allowed to drive into Moscow on the following day. We had an impromptu meeting in which our leader explained the situation and announced we were leaving the next morning and drive into Moscow. Those who did not feel comfortable could stay behind (of course no one wanted to do that.) We went upstairs to our rooms. Some gathered to cut out crosses from cardboard disguised as suitcase liners, cut them into crosses, and wrote in Russian "Christos vosktresn" (Christ is risen, the greeting of the underground church) and hand wrote pamphlets in Russians quoting Biblical salvation messages. We were all up early the next morning. The lobby was filled with plains clothed policemen. When we exited the hotel, several them got up and headed to the telephones. We drove quite a distance before reaching a roadblock. They were shown our itinerary but denied us access and order us to park on the side of the road. During this time carloads of police arrived and blocked us in.

After a lengthy discussion, it became obvious we were not going to Moscow on this day. Our leader went to each van and said it had become obvious our outreach was to be here. We exited our vans, grouped up, and displayed our signs. Meanwhile more police showed up. Busloads of people heading to Moscow were allowed to pass on through. I recall one school bus drove by, and a young lady saw us, smiled, and pointed to heart as to indicate she was a believer. After a lengthy time, we were escorted by the police back to our hotel. When we arrived, the hotel was surrounded by the police. A crowd of people were gathered outside the police line. They nor us were not allowed to cross the line. Inside the hotel, our tour guide gathered us and announced that morning "we were so busy that we did not have time to eat" and that the hotel staff had prepared a meal for us. Later a member of the hotel staff approached one of our group, hugged her and crossed herself, indicating she was a believer.

It had been a late night and a long morning. I retreated to my room and took a nap. I was awakened by a noise and saw one of our tour guides in my room and thought to myself "this is it! They are coming for me!" A plain clothed police officer was also in my room *My first thought was they are going to take me away.* I was informed our group was scheduled to take a boat tour on the Volga river and all members of the tour group were required to participate. We loaded in our vans and escorted to a boat. Before the police chased everyone away, we were able to share the gospel with them.

Upon our return the crowds of people in the area were scattered by the police to avoid contact with us. That night we witnessed in the hotel to who we could and slept soundly. We felt sorry for the police circling the hotel outside that night as it was raining, and we had done what we set out to do and were not going anywhere. The next couple of days our tour continued, only we had our own police escorts assigned to keep away the Russians from us.

Our last night was to be spent in Novgorod. Suspiciously some people were allowed to cross the police line. We were instructed to stay inside the hotel. I recall sitting on a bench in a window overlooking the streets and watching the Russian people below. It was here; I made a commitment to God I would go wherever he would send me and do what he wanted me to do.

At dinner that night we were informed that we would be escorted out of the Soviet Union the following day, and local officials stated, "Their freedoms were not like the freedoms we had in the west!" He further stated, "If we were to continue to share the gospel and pass out our handwritten Bible tracts, that severe measures would be taken against us!"

The next morning, we were escorted out of the country by our Soviet police escort. I recall looking out my window in the van and observed above us. a horse driven chariot driven by an angel. For at least a half hour I kept looking and seeing it still there. I was hoping someone else would notice it. So, I did not want to think I was going nuts. As far as I know, I was the only one who saw this.

At the border we had a lengthy crossing as the soldiers searched everything and confiscated every roll of film they could locate. Fortunately, some film was not located.

Upon crossing into Finland, we pulled over to thank God and sang "Hallelujah, for the Lord our God the almighty reigns!!" We found a place to make overseas calls. It took an hour to connect with my mom in California. This was my first and only call on the historic underseas Atlantic cable. My mom was awakened from a sound sleep, but she was incredibly happy to hear my voice and learned we had a successful mission in the Soviet Union, But most of all. to learn we were safe and back in the free world. She later told me that the next day she was wondering if it had been a dream.

We retreated to the place where we had left our Bibles and had a wonderful meeting together, one brother read a scripture that stated, *"Had the Lord not been with us, our enemies would have consumed us."* I did not mention my Angel- chariot sighting.

The following day we boarded a ferry across the Baltic sea. Upon arrival in Stockholm, we went to the United States Embassy and made an official report of our outreach in the Soviet Union. We spent the night on a boat converted to a youth hotel on a river in the middle of the city. We received word from a reporter that our story had been posted on an international news source and teletyped all over the world. We also learned a news conference had been scheduled for us upon our return to London. One of the highlights for me was we camped in Holland while driving back to England, a little European car drove up and out came the infamous and my "spiritual hero", Brother Andrew (God's Smuggler). He informed us the Christian's across the Communist block had already heard about the public witness and were greatly encouraged. Also, he told us the Bibles smuggled in for us to hand out, had safely reached the Christians and had not been confiscated. We continued our journey on the following day and finally arrived back in London and had a press conference in an old cathedral. What joy it was to know this mission could be considered successful in that by the help of God, we were able to openly witness in the communist world, encouraged the persecuted Christians, and had the massive coverage in which the communist lie about freedom of religious belief had been exposed. It was difficult to go our ways and separate from our "Comrades in Christ." A detailed book entitled "Roadblock to Moscow" was written by Nick Savoca and was published by Fleming H. Revell Company.

Upon return to the United States, I rejoined my ministry team in

California. There were many opportunities to share our story in churches and various groups. We had numerous newspaper interviews and a radio interview. It was during this time some of my friend's gave me the nick name of "Brother Frank, God's Struggler"

After it was time for me to complete my school and my team dissolved, it was time to seek God for the next season of my life. I thought the Lord was Directing me to spend a summer mission in Northern Ireland. No doors opened and at one point I called an airline to see if a ticket had been purchased for me. It became obvious that was not going to happen and the Lord had something else for me.

One humorous incident I recalled that happened that summer is, I never experienced any fear during the outreach to the Soviet Union. But this one morning, I woke up at home and the thought came to me that I could have ended up in a Soviet Gulag Prison and the roommate of the infamous Russian freedom writer, Alexander Solschenizn.

This summer became a critical time of developing my Relationship with God and started my Journey in truly getting to know him and gain some understanding of his ways.

Upon My return, I wrote a letter to the President of the United States detailing the events while in the Soviet Union. One morning the telephone rang. It was for me. And a person Identified themselves as a ranking official from the White House in Washington D.C. He informed me a meeting was currently taking place with a diplomat from the Soviet Embassy in regards to my letter. I was overjoyed to learn my letter was receiving such high-level attention.

I got down on my knees and started thanking God. He spoke to me and instructed me to turn to Jeremiah 1:4-10; The Lord spoke to Jeremiah and said," *I have sanctified you and appointed you as my spokesman to the world.* I responded by saying I cannot do that! I am too young! (I was only 18 years old) ... The Lord instructed me to keep on reading. *Jeremiah also stated, "I can't do that! I am far to young! I'm only a youth!" God continued to say, "You will go wherever I send you and speak whatever I tell you to. Don't be afraid of the people, for I the Lord, will be with you and see you through".* I was thoroughly "Wowed" by this and had no idea where this would take me in life!

Prior to starting the Mobile Training School. My mother gave me a copy of the "Living Bible". For the first time in my life, I felt I could finally understand the word of God and many things became very real to me despite many people downgraded it because it was a paraphrased. But really, there were many sources to confirm things, and in my mind what good would "God's word" be to us if we could not understand it?

This summer was spent seeking God quietly (Psalm 46:10) *"Be still and know that I am God"* I also focused on developing my relationship with God. (Job36:26) *"God is Great, but we know him not".*

(Hosea 6:6) *"I don't want your Sacrifices-I want your love; I don't want your offerings-I WANT YOU TO KNOW ME!!* The big instruction for me was found in (II Peter 1:5-7)....*"You must learn to know God better and discover what he wants you to do! Next learn to put aside your own desires so that you will become patient and godly, gladly letting God have his way with you. This will make possible the next step which is for you to enjoy other people and to like them and finally grow to love them deeply".*

(Daniel 11:32) *"The people who know their God, shall be strong and do exploits"*

I spent that summer developing a relationship with my creator. I started a position at the local Youth With a Mission international office in their tape ministry "Truth Tapes International". I learned to run a cassette duplicator and later learned to edit and master teachings from the mission's international schools. Was like attending one of the schools itself, only more intense in that I had to go over the teaching's multiple times before the final master was complete.

Just prior to assuming my duties with Truth Tapes International, I attended a Youth With a Mission Spiritual leadership conference. One of the speakers talked on the "Greatness of God" She challenged us to ask God to show us how great and powerful he is. So... when I got home, I went to my knees and asked God to show me how great and powerful he is. To be honest I did not know what to expect. I kid you not, right after I asked God to show me how powerful he was, He sent a small earthquake. I really did not expect this! I thought He would prompt a "mind blowing scripture or impress someone to telephone me with a prophetic message of sorts. However, he shook the ground for me. I was flabbergasted and rather speechless.

I worked at Truth Tapes International for approximately one year. We sent teaching cassettes and mastered/edited tapes all over the world.

One day the director walked into my office and introduced me to a fellow named Mike from Youth with a Mission's South Africa's tape ministry. Me and my great knowledge of geography, I asked him, "Which country?" Not knowing in a few years God would send me there. . One morning while editing a lecture. A Filipino fellow from the print room, walked in and asked me to pray for him as he did not feel well. I laid hands on him and gave the best healing prayer I had. The way he looked and sounded, I expected him to go home and go to bed. A few minutes later, to my surprise He came back and thanked me for the prayer, He said he was feeling much better! The following summer of 1974, Youth with a mission had a summer outreach in Spokane, Washington at the world's fair. My boss asked me to drive a van up there with the outreach cook from Norway. He was remarkably interesting. He had cooked for the king of Norway, Presidents of the United States, and learned English by reading smuggled English newspapers during World War II. After traveling with him for three days, I was able to translate his broken English. After the outreach, I returned back to my position at Truth Tapes International.

Subsequently I was asked to speak at a weekend youth camp at Zacca Lake, California. It was my custom to spend twice as much time in prayer for each session I was to speak at. While walking around the Lake, praying, The Lord told me he wanted me to attend a School of Evangelism in Lausanne Switzerland (Ecole le Foret, School of languages,-cultures. and evangelism).

CHAPTER 5

THE CUCKOO BIRDS

I gave notice to my boss at Truth Tapes International, trained my replacement, and found employment as a mechanical assembler to earn funds for my next adventure. I did my best to earn funds for school. During this time. I learned the meaning of; "When we do our best, God does the rest!" It was getting close to sending in my application with an application fee. My older brother showed up at my house with a check one afternoon. He informed me he and his wife felt led to give me some money for this school. I was able to send in my application with the fee and had some left over. Over time my church deacon board contributed some funds as well as my parents. It was not enough to cover all the expenses, but enough to confirm it was God's will for me to go. I also was able to save some from my employment.

Prior to my departure, my dad handed me some cash to obtain a motel room in Vancouver, Canada, so I did not have to sleep in the airport on my first night of my travels. That night I felt rather lost. I did not know when I would be coming back home, and I was alone. I cried that night and called home. The next day I was fine and caught my next flight to Toronto. On the flight from Toronto to Switzerland was at night, I had a row to myself and I was fed New York steak. Really had the feeling of a King's kid.

I was awakened the next morning to an announcement of breakfast and that we were 30,000 feet above Scotland (The land of my ancestors).

After landing in Geneva, Switzerland, I followed the instructions mailed to me. Caught a train to Lausanne, traveled along the shores of the infamous Lake Geneva, located the bus that would take me down the road from the school.

The ride along the Swiss countryside was more beautiful than I could imagine. I walked from the bus stop, carrying my suitcase and arrived at the school. It was a multi-story building that had once been a hotel. Had old fashion Swiss design.

I walked into the lobby and was escorted to the admission's office. I was greeted by a staff member and was invited to sit down to discuss business. I was informed I owed more money for tuition upon arrival than I had on my person. I was told the money was due at his time. I responded by stating,

"God had directed me there and provided so far and would provide for the rest." I gave him what funds I had available on my person.

I had this feeling I was going to be sent home (thank God I purchased a round trip-ticket). To my relief, I was told, "We will be praying for you!" Wew!!! What a relief!!! He gave me a copy of the schedule and in-house rules, then escorted me to my room.

My room was three floors upstairs. It was room 32, later to be called "room dirty two" as one of my roommates was rather unkempt. The room had a wonderful view of the Italian Alps.

One of my roommates was a youth leader of a large Pentecostal denomination and my other roommate was a young fellow originally from the United States whose parents were Baptist missionaries to Israel. We would spend 3 months together during the lecture phase of this school. Here I was a fellow from a non-denominational background. Perfect match!!

The lecturers came from many backgrounds and different ministry types. The average lecturer had one week. The speakers included "Floyd McClung" whose ministry had been to the hippy-.counterculture; Brother Andrew (God's Smuggler) whose ministry was to the underground church behind the borders of Communist countries; Gordon Olson, was the in-house theologian. Mr. Olson had an interesting story in that he was a minister and was preaching common theology (i.e., predestination, unconquered sin, etc.). One day he was preaching and noticed a Bible verse on the back wall; Jesus said, "*Behold I stand at the door and knock. Whoever will open the door, I will come in!*" (Rev.3:20). Instead of questioning God and/or back sliding, He gave up his ministry, became an engineer for a tractor company and spent his life reading and researching the Bible and it's interpreting scholars.

When he started, he was slow and monotone? By the time he finished he became so excited I thought he would drop dead of a heart attack. Unlike most theologians I had been exposed to, He ended his lectures by stating, " Don't just believe what I have taught you. Get down on your knees, prayer fully study the Word of God and come to your own conclusions!" This was a blessing to me as what he taught made a lot of sense (unlike others I had heard on the same subject matter),

Another lecturer was a Scotsman, named Campbell McAlpine, He taught about reading scripture, meditating on it and giving it some thought.

One instructor was Jean Darnell. She taught all week long and had a unique ministry for praying and prophesying over each student. When it became my turn to be prayed for. She laid hands on me, paused, and stated, "you are going to be a fisher of men, (at this point I was rather skeptic as we all are called to be fishers of men) as she continued, She further stated, "to many types of men in many different ways".

How right she was!! Over time I saw 25 different countries. preached, taught the word, was an evangelist, smuggled Bibles, did deputation work, acted in Christian plays, worked in a Christian video studio, taught street drama, wrote plays, worked with youth and adults, performed voice overs, wrote music, led worship, produced slide presentations to be shown behind Christian musicals, coordinated stage crews and a sound engineer for Christian music groups, was a camp counselor and a speaker, Wrote children's stories, Taught a Sunday School class, a Mobile Intensive Care Unit Paramedic, a Correctional Officer fot 18 years, A Probation Officer for 10 years assigned to the Court Investigative Unit. etc.

Across the street from the school was a forest. I spent much time there walking, praying, and thinking about the things I was learning. I learned to appreciate God's handiwork and design. I was amazed how much thought God put into His creation.

Our day at the school started with breakfast, quiet time, split into groups for intercessory prayer, Lectures, lunch, designated duties around the school (I was assigned to cassette duplicating duties), Had some free time, dinner, then our nightly lectures. I loved walking in the forest afterwards communing with God and hashing over the evening lectures, then to bed.

Saturdays were mostly free with a "love feast" that evening. We had to dress in our best, had a nice meal, and a time of sharing and worship. I usually took the bus into town in the morning to purchase some necessities, bought a hot dog, and stopped into a candy store where the proprietor spoke every language but English,

On Sundays we went to churches in town. We had three choices. I went to a small English speaking Catholic church. It was a small congregation of mostly United Nations employees. The priest was from Ireland. He had a long white beard, wore a robe that resembled a white flower sack. He had us from the school sing scripture chorus's in the beginning of each service. The rest of the day was quiet and spent fellowshipping with other students and writing letters. If I recall right, our weekly lecturer for that week started on Sunday nights.

The three-month lecture phase went quickly. Soon it was time for the next phase, the middle East field trip. I was still waiting for God's provision for the lecture phase. I prayed and decided it was best to head back home to get a job and pay off my lecture phase tuition. While in prayer the night before I was supposed to leave the Lord said informed me," that if I was asked to stay and work on staff, I was to do so".

The following day a brother was going to drive me to the airport.

While saying my goodbyes with my suitcase in hand; the director of the school met me in the hall. He asked me where I was headed. He further asked me to pray and work with their video ministry.

So... there it was the next phase of my spiritual service adventure. I went back to my room, unpacked, and subsequently saw my fellow students head off to the middle East.

It was rather quiet for a short time until the next group of students arrive for their school. My new roommates were a Swiss-German fellow and a brother from New Zealand

While waiting for the arrival of the next class. I was in my room cleaning and there was a knock on my door. When I opened the door, no one was there. I looked down on the floor and there was a note addressed to me. I opened it. It was from the school accounting office informing that the balance of my tuition had been paid off! To this day, I do not know who God used, but needless to say I was extremely overjoyed to receive this news.

During this break, a staff member from Canada asked me to join him on a weekend backpack trip to the Swiss Alps. I could not turn down this opportunity. We managed to gather some Backpacking equipment from the basement and my new Swiss roommate lent me a sleeping bag he thought was a warm down bag.

When the day arrived to leave, we drove through the alps, saw tank traps embedded in the road to protect the country from invaders there were also there were landing strips built inside the mountains and we saw fighter jets take off from there. It was fascinating. We parked, found the marked trail and started our hike up hills into the alps. I saw herds of cattle and flocks of sheep. We also passed several shepherd huts. We located our camp site in a small valley at the foot of a glacier. I awoke early to the morning song of the infamous "Cuckoo bird". I did not realize they were for real. I was also very cold and learned my sleeping bag was Dacron, not Down, as previously thought. We had breakfast, packed up, hiked up the other hill and viewed a beautiful Swiss valley. There was an old village with a castle dating from 1200, a chocolate factory and the infamous Gruyeres cheese factory

After returning back to the school I was asked to help with a Swiss family retreat. I was to oversee the younger children. My interpreter was a young 5-year-old who was fluent in several languages. This was a nightmare for me. My young interrupter was excellent!!! At one-point things got out of hand and an older swiss man came in and chewed out the children. I decided at this time this not my ministry. The school got back into full swing. Was fun working the video camera during the lectures and meeting new students from other parts of the world and different backgrounds and cultures. This class had many of the same lecturers and some we did not have previously. Including Winkie Pratney (my favorite Christian Apologist). A singing group from New Zealand, call "Scripture in Song"). I learned much from them in what worship is. I learned the difference between Worship and Praise. Another speaker from New Zealand, Reona Peterson. She had been arrested in Albania for passing out Bibles. She was sentenced to be executed by a firing squad but was released at the border with her belongings on the day of her scheduled execution. Was an incredible story.

One afternoon my New Zealand Roommate and I climbed out the window onto the roof and braced ourselves on the heavy-duty snow railing. Sitting way below us was a student from Olympia, Washington, named Dallana Pucket. We loudly whispered; "Dallana!!!! Go to Albania". We later discovered she heard us and at the time was asking God at what she should do after she completed the school. She never made it to Albania, but later went to Africa.

Another rememberable event took place on a rare warm evening in front of the school. There was a ruckus in front of the school. Someone had found hedgehog. I had never seen one in person. It was a cute little prickly critter infested with lice.

One fine warm Swiss day, a friend from Canada and I were assigned to show a guest around the town of Lausanne. After viewing an historical castle, we walked the shores of Lake Geneva. My friend shouted out, "Look! There is Francis Schaeffer (an infamous American Theologian and Philosopher), !

He was wearing lederhosen's and was talking with man wearing a very fashionable suit. Mr. Schaeffer paused to talk with us. What a blessing to meet him.

While at the school, I met Christians from various parts of the United States, Canada, New Zealand, Australia, Thailand, England, Norway, Holland, The Republic of South Africa, Rhodesia, Ethiopia, Norway, Switzerland, Germany, and Scotland. Had a true international atmosphere not to mention students from various Christian backgrounds. We had two Mennonites from different parts of the United States. I had heard of them but never met any.

It coming to the close of this school, when one night the Lord spoke to me in a dream and instructed me to go to South Africa. I do not remember any details of this dream other than waking up the next morning believing this was to be my next move. I continued to pray about it and wrote the director at Ywam South Africa. He responded and appeared excited to have me come and use my skills in their developing tape ministry (South Africa's version of "Truth Tapes").

I flew back to the United States via Canada to prepare for this new ministry in a foreign land., This time I spent a memorable night in the Vancouver, Canada airport, sleeping on an airport bench. It took some adjusting to being back home. As doors opened, I was involved in my home church. I was hired to work at a Christian publishing/distributor company that I had work for off and on since my High School days.

As far as preparation for Africa all I could do was pray and continued via letters to communicate with the director in South Africa. I also research for economical ways to reach my destination in Africa. I learned of obtaining transport on Ships to Africa. This sounded adventurous to me. But the time frames did not work with the mission's schedule. A person working for International Youth With A Mission office nearby made a ministry of finding affordable transportation for its members and did so for me.

CHAPTER 6

THE RUMBLE IN THE JUNGLE

I once heard someone say, " Jesus said, We are to go into the world to preach the Gospel". He never mentioned anything about us coming back! I was excited to have God want me to do anything or go anywhere for him (Psalm 40:8) " *I delight to do thy will oh Lord.*" In this event I did not know if or when I would be coming back home.

The day before my departure for Africa, I was called up to the front my church, The pastor and others gathered around me, laid hands on me and prayed for me. They then sang the song, *"It is the Lord who goes before You.!!"*

The following day I boarded an airliner to Frankfort, Germany. I had a week before my flight from Luxembourg flew me to Johannesburg, South Africa. I really had no idea what to do during that week. When I arrived in Germany. A little prayer goes a long way. After I landed, I went up to an airline desk to explore flights to Switzerland. I ended up on a Spanish airline making a special unscheduled flight to Geneva. I may have been the only passenger on board.

I caught the train to Lausanne, got off and decided to face a fear. I was going to try escargot (snails)! I walked up to a restaurant, looked at the menu on the window, turned away and walked to my favorite hotdog stand. I then caught the bus to the school I previously attended. I got off, checked into a motel down the road. I then enter my old ala mater and was welcomed with open arms. I fellowshipped there for several days before continuing to Africa.

It was not to long before I found myself on a flight to Luxembourg. Before landing I recall seeing a lot of castles.

My flight to Africa left in the evening so I missed a lot of scenery. During the night we landed in The Congo to refuel. We were allowed to disembark and walk into the terminal. We were warned not to purchase the high- priced beverages as the airlines would provide free beverages when we reboarded the aircraft. There were lots of guards roaming around armed with AK-47 automatic weapons wearing Russian military uniforms. The restroom was covered in fecal matter; it was really disgusting!!! We finally boarded and departed.

Upon Arrival in Johannesburg, I telephoned the number given to me. Who should arrive to greet me? But Mike! The fellow I met in California from South Africa several years prior.

The base was in the country outside a village called "Halfway House". It was between Johannesburg and Pretoria. The village had a small store, a branch of Barkley's Bank, and a snake park. The school facilities appeared to have been a mansion at one time. It was perfect for a school. Lots of rooms, out buildings, a swimming pool; all centered on a large plot of land.

I was taken inside, introduced to the director from Scotland, shown my workplace; a humble recording booth with minimal equipment, and shown my quarters in the men section. It was a building approximately 50 yards from the main building with two large bedrooms that housed 6 staff members each. A bathroom was outside, in between the staff housing. It was extremely cold in the winter after getting out of the showers.

I met a family there I had met in Switzerland. Frikki, June, and their two children. What a happy reunion!!! Frikki once told me, "Once you have tasted African water, no other water will satisfy". The truth was when you left Africa you would miss it.

They took me on a venture the following week to expose me to the Afrikaans culture, a real South African "Braai" (their version of a bar-b-Que). I was introduced to a greeting in their culture with no briefing. When we arrived at their friend's home, we were greeted by their two attractive-older teen daughters. When introduced, they both came up and kissed me on the lips! I thought to my young self, "Wow! I am going to like it here!"

Years later I learned Frikki and his family moved to California to Pastor a church several hours from my home. Sadly, we learned he went back to South Africa for a visit and died in a car accident. I wish we had known sooner as he was just a few hours from us. I would have loved to reacquaint with him and his family and hear him do his stuff from the pulpit.

I quickly learned of the perplexed situation in this young country labeled "Apartite". The two dominate white cultures here, had hard feelings towards each other (English and Afrikaans). The whites disliked the black tribal cultures. Many blacks did not like the whites. To top that off many of the African tribes disliked each other. Just when you thought it could not get any worse, there was another group called the "Colours", people from cross breeding of whites, blacks, etc. There was a lot of deeprooted hate and bitterness. Not to mention the current racial unrest and a communist sponsored terrorist war on the borders and surrounding countries. A place ripe for spiritual awakening and renewal. The majority of the students at the school were English and Afrikaners. The law of Apartite dictated "Whites Only". Many here learned to pray for others, learned to love different races through God's eye's, and learned forgiveness.

During the current lecture phase, the director asked me to accompany the assistant director on a trip to South West Africa (now referred to as Namibia) while the field trip was being planned and he thought I could see and experience more of Africa and it's cultures.

It was an interesting venture seeing the African wildlife in the bush. We also drove through the Desert. Sand dunes as far as the eye could see and glimpses of the natives who managed to survive in this environment.

I got a realistic view of the terrorist war one night when we were pulled over by the military and searched, as a family of farmers nearby had been killed that night by terrorists. That night we drove further, pulled over in the bush and slept peacefully. I recall waking up to a spectacular sight and seeing the sun rising over the bushveld.

We visited an YWAM supporter while scheduling meetings. I was looking through their library and found a book on the snakes in southern Africa. One snake stood out was called a "night adder". A very poisonous snake that came out at night and lay on the warm asphalt roads. It would strike with no warning. So much for my night walks on the road.

Before leaving South West Africa. We visited a friend of my traveling partner. He took us on a night hunt in the bush. We drove through the bush with bright spotlights. We got one small Spring bok. Now when I look back, I do not think that was a good idea as most terrorist attacks seem to take place in the bush at night.

Upon arriving at the school, the director asked me to assemble and train a street drama group for outreach and to perform at meetings. I recruited two volunteers to do a sample performance in front of the school to find volunteers to form a group. I got a good response. Most of the skits were comic in origin but ended with a powerful message.

During one practice session, I was teaching a comical dance routine to accompany a song. One Afrikaans girl was having a difficult time mastering the steps. When she finally got it, I said "very good" in Spanish. At this time everyone busted out laughing and literally started rolling on the ground and the girl I complimented turned red. I found out this term in Spanish closely resembled the Afrikaans words for "Nice Legs"!

When the night sessions were over, I like to stretch out on the diving board at the pool and look up into sky. I was looking into the southern hemisphere (I don't know if it was any difference than the northern hemisphere.) I would see the planets, the countless stars, constellations and would be in awe how big the universe was, and the fact God was much bigger; Yet he could be interested in each of us individually, so small compared to the bigger picture.

I was appointed to go on the African field trip to assist the leader. We camped out every night. One night we stayed at a Christian retreat. While helping organize the camp, some of the students opted to take a hike on a mountain overlooking us. You could hear baboons grunting up there. They were lively creatures and an encounter with them was not something you wanted to do. The baboons had been known to get hostile, bite you, and or throw rocks at you. When the students returned, one reported on the way up the hill, a cobra snake jumped up from behind a rock.

Fortunately, it did not attack anyone. We stayed with a YWAM supporter I had visited previously. There were no shower facilities available, but there was a swimming pool that had not been attended to in a long time. It was green and slimy. I was getting desperate, I put on my swimsuit and prayed there was no creatures or blood sucking leeches in there. I swam with Olympic speed and made it to the other side with no incidents or leeches dangling from my extremities.

One night I was appointed to lead worship for an outdoor meeting. We had a guest speaker flown in for the night. While we were worshiping, the presence of the Lord was strong. I felt led to have the students pray with each other. The Lord started an obvious work amongst the students. The guest speaker sensed it and gave up his time to allow the Holy Spirit to continue the work He started. We headed north from there to the Angolan border. We camped at some fairgrounds that were used to house refugees from war torn Angola. One night the group was headed out to hold a meeting at a local church. I was assigned to stay behind and guard the camp. It was just me with no weapons of defense. Thank God nothing happened. I walked around all night to make sure there was no unwelcome visitors. There was a wedding going on with the refugees. It was so tempting to leave my post and invite myself to this happy occasion with people who had suffered so much. But I remained on duty.

Heading down south, we traveled on the coast. There were sand dunes east of us and the Atlantic Ocean to the west of the road We stopped to go swimming. While swimming in the water we saw a bunch of fins swimming towards us. Our first thought it might be some of Africa's killer sharks. We got out of the water as quickly as possible. We were relieved to discover they were dolphins.

After entering back into South Africa, we stopped at an Ostrich park. We were given the opportunity to ride one and participate in a race. That was an incredible experience!

We drove down to the most southern end of South Africa, Cape Town. We stayed at Mowbray Presbyterian Church. I spent a lot of Time alone with God, praying and worshiping in the old belfry. I had a blessed opportunity to speak their youth group one night, the group's ages ranged from young teenagers to university students. I spoke for over an hour on

"Knowing God". I seemed to hold their attention and They seem to enjoy it. I was invited to speak to their next youth group meeting and was given a topic; "New life in New Wine skins". This was new experience for me.

Usually when I was invited to speak it was to be on whatever the Lord laid on my heart. Fortunately, I had a week to prepare. I was familiar with The scripture referring to this topic. One day while walking around the neighborhood, I spotted two empty wine bottles against a fence, and a seemingly brilliant idea popped in my head!

I marked one bottle "New Wine skin" and the other bottle "Old Wine skin". I explain what happened when new wine (I used Kool aide) was poured into an old wine skin (it would explode). I caused the old wine skin to explode by placing a towel over it over a plastic container and struck it with a hammer. I then explained about the changes in our life when we asked Jesus into our lives. The message seemed to get across and make a difference.

Upon return to the school, a team was being formed to conduct a weekend multi-racial conference in Rhodesia. I was picked to be a part of the team. A full-fledged terrorist war was going on that country because of their racial policies, so special precautions were in place.

Upon entrance into the country, there was a zone that required an armed military escort. The few houses we passed in the area had tall chain linked fence with razor and or electric fence and were accompanied with large-mean looking guard dogs. We passed a vehicle broke down with two young fellows armed with hand grenades. The outside world had placed financial restriction on Rhodesia there was a lack of modern amenities. In the capital, the roads were dirt. It was common to see horse driven wagons driving through the capital and old cars collectors in the United States would die for! The camp was held at a retreat site on Lake Macoway. There were signs warning of a parasite on the shoreline known as Bilharzia. We took a kayak ride and did fine until we reached the shoreline and fell in. With my limited knowledge of African exotic diseases. I figured the worst-case scenario was a sleeping sickness. I determined that was my spiritual gift anyway. After I returned to the states, I was feeling weak. I explained to the doctor what I had been exposed to. She walked me into the laboratory and pulled out a book that showed a picture of a fellow with elephantiasis of the testicles. She asked me if I had that problem. I responded with a resounding, "NO"! If I had known that I would have stayed a mile away from the lake.

The camp went well. There was a big, tall muscular fellow there who used to be a terrorist until he gave his life to Jesus.

On our way home at the border, we stopped at a gas station. I walked into the bushveld and behold, there was a big male lion in front of me. Did I mentioned he was caged up? Makes for a good story.: Sadly, upon our returned to our base. We learned a mission station on the Mozambique/ Rhodesian border was attacked by Terrorist and slaughtered everyone. Sad, as these wonderful people would have helped anyone.

Upon returned to the base, all the students were assigned to teams for summer of service. I was attached to a team going to the small African nation of Lesotho.

We spent a short time at a career missionary's home at the border of Lesotho and the Republic of South Africa. One day a truck that resembled a small dump truck arrived. We loaded our stuff in the back, hopped in the back, and off we went onto an unpaved road. We climbed into the mountains and came to a small village of mud huts with thatched grass roof. We stopped at a hut that was to be where we would stay and work from. During our first days, the local village chief arranged an outdoor meeting with the villagers to give us a formal greeting and welcome. It was on the chilly side. During the welcome ceremony, the local witch doctor arrived with no shirt, exposing his big belly. We were told it was his way of showing his power in the cold.

During the day, we would ride small horses called Lesotho ponies to surrounding villages for meetings with believers and for evangelistic meetings. In the evenings we held indoor meetings at our huts for local believers. On some of these moons lit nights many locals would walk as far as five miles to attend. Their music was incredible. There was a unique blend and harmony of angelic sounding voices. I wish we had the means to record it.

On one night it was my turn to speak. It was fun working with an interrupter. I had to speak slowly and clearly. When I injected my style of humor, the interpreter would stop, look at me, and proceed. On several occasions he would burst out laughing when it later processed in his head what U said.

One morning we were asked to pray for a local elderly man in the village who was ill. We went to his hut, laid hands on him, and prayed our best healing prayers.

He died the following day and soon we watched his funeral procession pass our hut. I found this disheartening. Funny how God works. The villagers were blessed as they thought we prayed that he would die, as it turned out to be his wishes.

Before leaving Lesotho, we were on our daily rounds and ran into another ill villager. My first thought was, I hope our leader doesn't volunteer our healing prayers. Sure enough, he did! Never heard the outcome of this prayer session.

Soon our time had come to leave. Our truck picked us up and down the hill we went. We later learned it had snowed after we left.

Soon it was Christmas time. It was my first Christmas away from home. Christmas was always a big deal with my family. I spent Christmas with my Afrikaans friends. We went to church. We sang some Carols, but there were no decorations, I went to a farm and we had a braai (a bar-b que). It was summer in this part of the world.

The next group of students arrived a month later. The school had a speaker from Switzerland. His name was Rudy Lack. He was Youth With A Mission's official international deputizer. He traveled around the world speaking and recruiting. After his lecture series was complete, I was invited to join him on a world wind tour of South Africa. It was a great opportunity to learn some more speaking and recruiting skills. Once again, I was blessed to share at the Mowbray Presbyterian Church.

While en route back to the YWAM base at Halfway house, the Lord spoke to me and told me it was time to go back home to California. No reason, no further direction. I shared my direction with the leader. He did not seem incredibly happy.

Soon all the arrangements were made to travel back. When the day came to leave, a large group of my friends came to the airport to see off. They prayed for me and sang a lively African song(*Sa hamba Utina Ahum Shaba*) and off I went. The flight landed in Kenya to refuel and off load some passengers. My last day in Africa. I was sad to leave this land that I had come to know and love. I spent one night in Brussels, Belgium and then back to land of my birth. (yes, I did miss Africa and its water!)

I put together a slide presentation on the Africa situation I entitled "Rumble in the Jungle". When the opportunities to show the presentation stopped. I volunteered to work at my home church with the youth, supervised the traveling youth choirs stage crews, and taught a ninth grade Sunday school class. Sometime during this, I went to Lake Isabella, rented a Motel room, and fasted and prayed about my next move. The Lord made it plain there was to be a slight change in my calling and direction in my life, with no specifics.

As much I enjoyed my work at my church, I felt a little disoriented but stayed focused on what was before me. Sometimes I felt like maybe somewhere I had failed God. But I stayed true to my God and focused on the task at hand.

During this time God blessed me in a special way. My mother told me of a fund-raising dinner with "Open Doors", (An Eastern European Mission), was having locally. My mother and I attended the dinner and I learned about a short-term mission programs they had. My heart and prayers still focused on the suffering church behind the Communist Iron Curtain. I prayed seriously about it and felt "the go ahead" to apply. To my joy, I received a letter of acceptance and more information.

To confirm this move, the Lord opened up a job with a small production company that had a contract with the "McDonald's' Hamburger chain" to provide props for on location shows Of "Miles of smiles" internationally for 50 "Ronald McDonald's" (McDonald's Spokesman clown).

I was hired to be the props director. Over the summer I was given a van, a shop to work in, and unlimited time to fulfill the contract. After building all the magic props needed, I was assigned to help build sound systems for the show.

The fellow I was assigned to work with was a professional sound engineer who recorded many popular Christian artists at the time and was responsible for the sound of the "Billy Graham" evangelistic crusades. I learned a lot during this time and felt very honored to work with this fellow.

As this contract dwindled down, it became time to go back overseas for the next Mission for my Lord.

As a result of this job, all the funds I needed were provided.

CHAPTER 7

GOD'S STRUGGLER RIDES AGAIN.

My letter of instruction arrived, detailing how to get to the training base in Holland, and some Dutch coins to use for the telephone for when I arrived at the appointed train depot.

All the instructions read like something out of a spy movie, but due to the nature of this type of work, secrecy was extremely important!

Before I left, my church called me up front, prayed for me, and sang the infamous "It is the Lord who goes before you!" I don't recall much about the flight. When I arrived in Amsterdam airport, I followed the instructions. Got to the train station alright and got on the right train. I was in awe on the train ride that God would call me to this type of mission and no idea what would happen and where I would end up. The train stopped at the depot I was to get off at. It was a covered concrete platform with a pay phone. It was not manned, and I was the only one there.

I followed the instructions, and someone answered the phone and spoke English. I did not have to wait to long for someone to arrive and pick me up.

An older fellow arrived in an older European car and drove me through multiple villages on the infamous Holland Dykes. I also saw windmills.

We arrived at an old farmhouse in the middle of nowhere. I was introduced to the director, staff, and other participants. My quarters were in a loft shared with other male participants.

The first few days were spent in training, Bible Study, prayer and getting to know each other. In the afternoon I worked with a fellow from France assisting in building an expansion project . We also put on a floor project in a barn, tamping down sand and bricks on top. It was to be used to house smuggling vehicles.

I met an interesting Dutch fellow there, his father was a pastor during the Nazis occupation. He told me stories how his father snuck around during the night to visit his parishioners to encourage them. During his stories you could almost hear the Nazi troops marching on the dykes above the old farmhouse.

My Dutch friend went with me to visit a lady from my home church who was in Amsterdam doing missions work. It was an uplifting visit and a fun train ride.

Upon return to the farmhouse. I was assigned to a team to take Bibles to the Country of Romania.

My team consisted of two others. The only thing I knew of Romania that it was ran by the Communists, it was the land of Transylvania and Count Dracula.

The journey was as exciting as the destination and mission. While driving through Germany I was pulled over on the Autobahn for driving to slow in the slow lane (60miles per hour) The trooper spoke to me in German. The more I asked him in German if he spoke English, The angrier he became. Fortunately, my team leader was fluent in German and we were able to work it out. The trooper demanded we pay the fine on the spot. We had the currency on hand. I hope he did not pocket the money.

We camped along the infamous Danube river in the shadow of an old castle on the hill above us. At night, the castle was lit up. I awoke early in the morning and took a walk along the riverbank to pray. The water was evaporating and had a fog like appearance. Was the perfect scene to pray for our upcoming mission.

In order to get to Romania, we had to drive through the Country of

Hungary. I did not recall much about the border crossing, except it was not as intense as the one I experienced in the Soviet Union.

Budapest, Hungary's capital, was also colorful, and the girls were also dressed more colorful. We Toured this city. This was one of the most incredible cities I had recalled ever seeing.

As we crossed the border into Romania, it was uneventful, We prayed the "Bible Smuggler's Prayer"; 'Lord, please make seeing eyes blind". The Bibles were not discovered! We proceeded to the Romanian town of Cluj and set up camp.

That night we parked a few blocks away from our contact. We met with our interpreter and proceeded to our contacts apartment. Everything we did was done very discreetly as to not to attract attention. You did not know who was an informer or a member of the secret police. We had a wonderful time and fellowship with our contacts. Arrangements were made to deliver the precious Bibles on the following evening. We walked back silently in the dark to our vehicle, hoping and praying it was still there and intact. It was still there in one piece.

After a good night sleep and some prayer, we toured the old city of Cluj. We saw an old cathedral, very dark inside, with old carvings of Mary and Saints, and countless candles lit. Outside there were Gypsys selling some handmade wares.

We headed back to camp to prepare for the delivery of the Bibles to the Christians of the underground church.

That night we followed our spy like procedures to go to our contact's home. There we were introduced to a Christian Romanian who was to direct us to our Bible drop off location. Enroute, we were stopped by a policeman in the middle of the road. Our contact slid behind the back seat. We showed the officer our passports and he waved us on. When it was clear, our contact popped up and raised his hand to God in a gesture of thanks for God for his protection. We arrived at a farmhouse in the middle of nowhere. A gathering of Christians was in progress. We were taken to their cellar where we left bags of Romanian Bibles. I was amazed where the Bibles were hidden. Only our team leader knew where they were at and how to access them. We had around 1,000 (One Thousand) Bibles we delivered.

We hugged the Christians goodbye and proceeded back to our

contact in Cluj. To everyone's relief we passed where the police officer had been previously, and thanked God he was gone. We spent some time fellowshipping with our contacts and returned to our campground. The following day we started our journey back. We had one more mission to complete with a believer in Hungary.

Driving through Hungary we spotted a Farmer's Market. We purchased some tomatoes and homemade paprika. Tasted really good!!!

That night we contacted a believer in Hungary. We did the usual night contact thing. Only this time I was assigned to babysit our vehicle. I noticed two men dressed in the typical hats and trench coats associated with the "secret police". I laid on the back seat, prayed, used all the tools I learned in spiritual warfare. Soon I felt an incredible peace. I sat up, looked out the window, and noticed my visitors were gone! I had a hallelujah session before my teammates returned. They reported a successful contact.

Our journey back to Holland was uneventful. We continued to pray for our contacts and that the Bibles would safely end up in believers' hands.

We were almost back to the farmhouse when I spotted a McDonald's hamburger restaurant. I prayed the lord would lay it on the driver to stop there. We did stop!!! What a joy to my heart to enjoy my quarter-pounder meal. I even kept the disposable place mat for my scrap book at home. We soon arrived back at the farmhouse and gave our report.

The time to return back to the United States came to soon.

CHAPTER 8

WEDDING BELLS

D uring my flight back to Los Angeles, I was reflecting on my life and the mission I had just completed. My flight was over the Atlantic Ocean and I could see the icy polar route below. I was trying to figure out what my ministry was in God's kingdom. I had been on mission trips but was not called to one country as a missionary. I am a licensed minister but had not been called to pastor. I taught God's word but was not a teacher. I have shared the gospel and saw folks come to the Lord, but I was not an evangelist. I prayed for the sick and some were healed, and some died, but I did not have a healing ministry. It suddenly struck me! I am a "Soldier and servant of Christ!" A soldier prepares for a mission, completes the mission and returns to prepare for the next mission. It dawned on me that this was what God was doing with me. I was so excited about my prior missions and whole heartily looking forward to what was next.

When I arrived home, I shared about my mission, when the speaking opportunities fizzled out, I obtained employment. I continue to help with the youth at my church and use my creative-sound skills with the church's music group.

I was employed as a store detective at a local record store when the thought came to me; that because of my interest and apparent gift to work with youth, that maybe I should consider getting a college degree in Youth Ministry. An idea popped in my mind I should get summer employment at a church summer camp before I dove into the years of education.

It was rather late to be applying for summer camp employment, But I did anyway. I received two offers. One camp wanted me to supervise their dining room, and the other camp wanted me for a floating camp counselor for different age groups. I accepted the second offer at Hume Lake Christian Camps. It was a great summer and I even got paid.

I worked in the wagon train camp with the younger age group, the ranch camp with JR. High age, and with the high school camp. Every week was different, and I looked forward to learning my assignment on Saturdays after the camps left.

During the evening devotions in my covered wagon cabin, I learned nearby wagons were listening to my devotionals through the canvas walls that included stories of my work behind the iron curtain and Africa.

My last week of the summer, I was assigned to work with camp security. At the end of the summer season, I packed my guitar, my sleeping bag, and my suitcase onto my motorcycle. I drove off in the sunset rejoicing for the wonderful summer I had serving God at the camp.

The following morning, I woke up in my bed to a phone call from the Hume lake camp manager offering me a full-time position with their new full-time camp security. Evidentially when they decided to hire me, they saw me drive off on my motorcycle before they could talk to me. I accepted the offer and reported two weeks later.

I was assigned to be the assistant security chief. I worked under Dick Chenot, a retired Air Force Colonel and an outstanding Christian. It was a blessing to get to know him and his outstanding wife. During the off season there were mostly weekend camps and different projects to help with. I learned to drive and operate the camp's fire engine and was sent to a class to become an Emergency Medical Technician IA (EMT).

One unexpected event took place that I did not expect. I met the woman who became my wife, Janet from Santa Cruz, California. She had worked at the camp for two years in the camp accommodations division. We hit it off and spend a lot of time together daily. On the cold winter nights while patrolling the camp, I would stop by her and her roommate's cabin for warm refreshments and to warm up. She liked to cook, and I liked to eat. A perfect match!!

As time progressed, my supervisor approached me and asked if I was going to marry Janet. I replied that it had been in my thoughts and my prayers, but I had not saved up the money for the ring. He instantly replied, " I will loan you the money and no hurry to pay it back!" I told him I did not want to go in debt. He grinned and replied, " I see, you are not sure!"

A short time later, Janet and I talked and prayed about it and decided to go ahead with it. I approached my supervisor to see if he was serious about his offer. I went to his cabin and his wife was there at the time. They both broke out with big grins, he pulled out his checkbook and asked how much.!!

When I told him the anticipated amount, he asked if that was going to be enough (we knew of a discount jewelry store down the hill in Fresno and saw the wedding set Janet liked.) Dick wrote us out a check. H and his wife congratulated us and make offers to pray for us. At our first opportunity, Janet and I drove to Fresno to order her ring.

On the day we were to pick up the ring it had snowed. In route I had to put snow chains on her car. It was my first time to do this. It took over an hour. After I finished applying the snow chains, A snowplow drove by and cleared the road.

When we arrived back to Janet's cabin and were alone. I got down on my knees and officially proposed to her. She said, "Yes!!". When time allowed, we drove up to her parent's and asked for their Blessings/permission. After they said yes, it was official; We were engaged! We set a date for June that was compatible with our camp schedule. The wheels begin to roll fast. Many stepped up to the plate and wanted to help us (Because we were "poor" camp workers) A local Oroville Pastor volunteered to officiate the vows. His wife volunteered to make the cake, all for no charge. They had been missionaries to the African nation of Uganda and were kicked out of the country for their Christian work. My older brother designed and printed out the wedding invitations. My younger brother agreed to play the piano for the wedding and some friends from my home church, Jessie and Kathy offered to help with music. Things came together quick. Janet and her mother made the wedding dresses and the dresses for the wedding. The new camp director who was a camp speaker, a published author, and a licensed psychologist offered to do the pre-marital counseling. The camp assigned us a cabin in the sub-division to ready before our wedding. I was able to move in and Janet would come over and give it her special touch. It was already when we returned from our wedding. For our honeymoon, we did not have a lot of money, so we purchased camping equipment.

The day came quickly. I drove a family friend of Janet's to the wedding from town. She was concerned the wedding would start before us. She did not know I was the groom. I silently chuckled!!!! Another event was taking place in town during the wedding. The Ronald McDonald show I worked on prior to my mission in Romania was going on in Town. I never saw the actual show, but my wedding had priority.

Although it was extremely hot, the wedding went nicely. We had a nice turn out with a good number of guests for the distance everyone had to travel. We got a lot of nice gifts and money also. On our honeymoon we were able to stay several nights in motels as well as camp as we originally planned. We also had enough to repay the loan for the rings.

We arrived back at the camp for staff orientation. We were asked to stand, we were introduced, and warmly congratulated.

CHAPTER 9

THE MOVE TO OUR MOUNTAINS

W hen the time came for us to leave the camp, we had several options. Move to nearby Fresno, to the Los Angeles area where I was from, to Santa Cruz where Janet came from, or to Oroville where her parents lived. We prayerfully choose Oroville because we wanted to live in the mountains. After two weeks I was hired to work with an ambulance company in Sacramento.

Subsequently we purchased land across from my in-laws. Built a house and raised our four children here. I worked 7 years as an Emergency Medical Technician/Paramedic. I worked and trained in 3 California ghettos The highlights of this time were delivering Baby Jesus one fine Sunday morning in West Sacramento on a Sunday morning.. Later I obtained employment closer to home as a correctional officer with the local sheriff's office for 18 years. I was able to obtain my bachelor's degree in Criminal Justice and Church Ministry.

As a result, I was hired at the local Probation Department and assigned to the "Court Investigation Unit". For ten years I worked with the criminal Courts and Judges in assisting with Sentencing Recommendations before retiring after ten years. While living in the mountains, we were able to assist in ministry with several small churches, we met some incredible Christians who were deeply in tuned with God and had life stories that seemed to walk out of these mountain's rich history. Our friends became like family. We dropped in unannounced, spent holidays and special occasions with each other. During my service in Emergency services and as a peace officer, I worked long hours and shift work. My wife, Janet did an outstanding job managing the household and raising our children. Over time our children grew up, went their ways, married, had children, and blessed us with nine grandchildren. Our house has survived over the years and continues to serve us well.

In my lifetime, I realized my calling included not only my church related work, but also my time working on the ambulance as a paramedic for seven years, and 28 years in the criminal justice system. In 2019, Janet and I found ourselves in Moscow airport exactly 40 years and one week later to the day after I was detained by the KGB outside of Moscow and escorted out of the country for preaching the Gospel. We were en-route to a free Romania for a wedding of our youngest son to a Romanian girl he met on a church mission trip. What a joy to see the changes there in the post-communist era. I was blessed to openly speak several times in church services and witness young people openly worshiping God.

I will never forget observing the Berlin Wall come down and the Iron Curtain collapse. I could not help but wonder if my work and prayers had some small part in these events.

I also wondered how the ministries I was involved in (the cassette tapes, video productions, the Bibles I gave to African Christians, the Bibles I helped smuggled into the Communist world, and the people I talked personally to about God in personal and groups) would have and who would be influenced. These are things one would never know until I stand before God.

No matter how menial our service appears, I found it a joy to serve our God. The Psalmist said," *I delight to do thy will oh Lord*". (Psalms 40:8)

Also, I have been challenged by Matthew 20:28. Jesus said," *The son of man did not come to be served, but to serve, and give his life a ransom for many*". Our life and our callings are to be a service to God and his creation in whatever ways God determined.

To contact the author, he can be reached via
email fcandlish@hotmail.com.

Printed in the United States
By Bookmasters